The Peter Project

From Fisherman to Founder

A Bible Study by

Rev. Dr. Shawn P. Richmond &
Minister Elder Linda V. Lee

A GOSHEN PUBLISHERS BOOK   VIRGINIA

The Peter Project
From Fisherman to Founder

ISBN: #978-1-959702-38-2

Copyright ©2026 Richmond and Lee

Library of Congress Cataloging-in-Publication Data

Published in 2026 by:

GOSHEN PUBLISHERS LLC
10307 West Broad Street, #198
Glen Allen, Va 23060

www.GoshenPublishers.com

Our books may be purchased in bulk for promotional, educational, or business use. For inquiries, don't hesitate to get in touch with the publisher via email: Agents@GoshenPublishers.com.

First Edition 2026

Cover designed by Goshen Publishers LLC

Printed in the United States of America

All Scriptures are quoted from the English Standard Version of The Holy Bible unless otherwise noted.

for those who labor in the Lord

CONTENTS

INTRODUCTION

PETER WAS NOT AN IDEA. HE WAS A MAN.

Before Peter became a sermon, he was a fisherman.

Not symbolic.

Not romantic.

Actual.

His hands were not made for parchment but for rope. His days did not begin with prayer but with nets soaked in yesterday. He worked the Sea of Galilee the way working men always do: before dawn, without guarantees, with trust in weather that did not love him back.

Peter was not trained for theology. He was trained for survival.

Which is why he spoke too quickly and listened too slowly at first. Which is why he felt everything before he understood anything. Which is why he both believed wildly and failed memorably.

Jesus did not recruit from synagogues when He called Peter.

He recruited from boats.

Peter followed at once, without the good sense most people call wisdom.

There is no evidence that he considered the outcome. There is every indication that he considered nothing but the voice.

Peter was the disciple who answered first and learned later. He was the one who pulled Jesus aside, corrected Him, questioned Him, defended Him, denied Him, and returned to Him.

Always returned.

If there is one word that belongs to Peter, it is not strength.

It is return.

Peter returned from confusion.

From ego.

From fear.

From failure.

When others grew silent, he spoke. When others endured quietly, he made a scene. When others watched, Peter rushed. When others doubted privately, he did so publicly.

He was not subtle.

And God did not ask him to be.

Peter declared Jesus divine in one moment and denied knowing Him in the next chapter.

Not because he was fake.

Because he was afraid.

Fear, not faithlessness, is the shape of his greatest failure.

He did not deny Jesus because he stopped believing.

He denied Jesus because believing suddenly became dangerous.

And then the rooster crowed.

Not to humiliate him.

But to wake him.

Resurrection did not end Peter's story.

It restored it.

Jesus did not reassign him.

He reasked him.

Three times.

Do you love me?

Peter answered more cautiously than before.

Not because he loved Jesus less.

Because he knew himself better.

And then Jesus did something no failure expects.

He trusted him again.

Gave him people.

Gave him responsibility.

Gave him authority.

Not because Peter had proven perfect.

But because he had proven capable of return.

In the book of Acts, Peter is no longer impulsive.

He is bold.

No longer brash.

But burning.

He preaches the first sermon of the church not with elegance, but with history in his voice. He explains prophecy like a man who has lived its consequences. He confronts power with an old fisherman's honesty and a redeemed man's courage.

The one who once sank now steadies others.

The one who fled now stands.

The one who denied now declares.

And it is Peter, not Paul, not John, not any polished voice, who first announces that God has no favorites. That Gentiles belong. That history has cracked open wider than anyone imagined.

Peter, the fisherman, becomes the doorman of the gospel.

This workbook is not about success.

It is about discipleship.

Not about perfection.

But persistence.

Peter matters not because he never fell.

But because he got up believing Jesus still called him by name.

This study is for those who speak before they think.

For those who promise and then panic.

For those who love loudly and fail honestly.

For those who return.

Peter's story is not proof that leadership begins in confidence.

It is evidence that calling survives collapse.

You are not reading the story of a man who did not stumble.

You are studying the life of one who did.

And was still trusted with fire.

WHY STUDY PETER?

Peter is one of the most relatable and transformative figures in the Bible. His journey from fisherman to apostle, from failure to forgiveness, from follower to martyr, reminds us of God's power to change lives.

A LEADER AMONG EQUALS

From the moment Jesus called him, Simon Peter stood out among the Twelve. His name appears first in every list of the apostles (Matthew 10:2; Mark 3:16; Luke 6:14; Acts 1:13), signifying his prominence and leadership within the early community of followers. Peter was not merely the first to be called—he was the one who consistently spoke and acted on behalf of the group. He voiced the great confession, "You are the Christ, the Son of the living God" (Matthew 16:16), giving theological clarity to the disciples' growing faith. Yet he was also bold enough to rebuke Jesus when told of His coming death (Matthew 16:22). Peter's fearless speech made him both the mouthpiece of revelation and the mirror of human misunderstanding. Through him, the Gospels reveal that genuine leadership often arises through both faith and failure.

WITNESS TO THE INNER MYSTERIES

Among the Twelve, Peter, James, and John formed Jesus' inner circle. They were present at moments of extraordinary revelation that others did not witness. Peter stood beside Jesus when He raised Jairus's daughter from death (Mark 5:37). He climbed the mountain and saw the Lord transfigured in divine glory (Matthew 17:1–9). He entered the shadows of Gethsemane, hearing the Savior's anguished prayers (Matthew 26:36–46). These experiences positioned Peter not only as an observer of miracles but as a participant in the mystery of both divine power and human suffering. His privileged presence at these events prepared him for his later role as a foundational witness to Christ's identity and mission.

INTIMACY AND ACCESS TO THE MASTER

Peter's closeness to Jesus was also personal. The Lord entered Peter's home and healed his mother-in-law (Mark 1:29–31), taught from Peter's fishing boat (Luke 5:3), and called him to walk upon the water (Matthew 14:29)—a feat no other disciple attempted. Even after Peter's denial, the resurrected Christ appeared to him privately before appearing to the rest (Luke 24:34; 1 Corinthians 15:5). These moments reveal the depth of their relationship: Peter knew the nearness of Christ's compassion and correction more intimately than any of the others. His life was the canvas upon which divine grace painted both human weakness and heavenly mercy.

TRANSFORMATION IN PUBLIC VIEW

Peter's spiritual growth unfolded openly before the eyes of the world. He began as a fisherman on the Sea of Galilee (Luke 5:1–11), became the confessor of faith (Matthew 16:16), faltered in fear by denying Jesus (Luke 22:54–62), and was publicly restored by Christ beside the sea (John 21:15–19). On the day of Pentecost, he rose as the courageous preacher whose sermon brought three thousand souls into the Church (Acts 2:14–41). Unlike the quiet maturation of other disciples, Peter's transformation was recorded in detail so that generations might see that grace can redeem even the most visible failures. His journey embodies the gospel truth that restoration is never beyond reach.

A FOUNDATIONAL WITNESS OF THE CHURCH

After the resurrection, Peter emerged as the visible leader of the early Church. He healed the lame (Acts 3:6–10), confronted corruption (Acts 5:1–11), opened the gospel to Gentiles through Cornelius (Acts 10), and defended the inclusion of all believers at the Jerusalem Council (Acts 15).

In each of these moments, Peter bridged the gap between the Jewish roots of faith and the global mission of the Church. Jesus' words, "On this rock I will build My Church" (Matthew 16:18), found fulfillment as Peter's ministry established the foundation of a new spiritual household uniting Jews and Gentiles under Christ.

A DEATH THAT SPOKE OF HUMILITY

Church tradition holds that Peter met his death in Rome under Emperor Nero, crucified upside down at his own request because he felt unworthy to die in the same manner as his Lord. His martyrdom completes the arc of a life that began with impulsive ambition and ended in profound humility. The fisherman who once feared the waves ultimately surrendered his life in the service of the One who calmed them.

SUMMARY: THE ROCK OF TRANSFORMATION

Peter's uniqueness among the disciples lies in his proximity, personality, and perseverance. He stood closest to Jesus in both glory and suffering; he spoke most frequently and most fervently; he failed most visibly and was restored most completely.

Through Peter, we see that leadership in God's kingdom is not reserved for the flawless but for the faithful—those willing to follow, fall, and rise again by grace. His life remains a living testimony that Christ can turn ordinary people into extraordinary instruments for His Church.

This study will help us trace Peter's journey in six stages: his background, his calling, his growth, his restoration, his legacy, and his role in building the church.

LEARNING OBJECTIVES

- Week 1: Peter's Background – Identify Peter's family, occupation, and cultural context, and explain how God calls ordinary people.

- Week 2: Peter's Call – Explain Peter's call to discipleship and apply the lessons of obedience.

- Week 3: Peter's Growth – Recognize Peter's strengths and weaknesses and understand how God uses both in shaping His people.

- Week 4: Peter's Restoration – Describe how Jesus restored Peter and apply principles of forgiveness.

- Week 5: Peter's Legacy – Summarize Peter's ministry and letters, and articulate lessons of faithfulness and endurance.

- Week 6: Peter and the Church – Explain Peter's role in the foundation of the early church and how believers today continue to build.

WEEK 1:
THE BACKGROUND OF PETER,
AN ORDINARY MAN CHOSEN BY GOD

THEME

God uses ordinary people to accomplish extraordinary purposes.

KEY SCRIPTURES #1, MATTHEW 4:18-20

> *"¹⁸ While walking by the Sea of Galilee, he saw two brothers, Simon (who is called Peter) and Andrew his brother, casting a net into the sea, for they were fishermen.*
>
> *¹⁹ And he said to them, "Follow me, and I will make you fishers of men."[a]*
>
> *²⁰ Immediately they left their nets and followed him."*

LET'S TALK ABOUT IT

Why is it that we will listen to others and immediately respond, react, or complete a task? Yet, when you have prayed for God to direct your steps, for God to open a closed door, for God to provide direction, and when you hear the voice of God, when the Holy Spirit gives you a revelation or insight, you ponder if it's the voice of God, the will of God, or the direction from God. You ask for another sign or wonder.

You question why God said what He said. Maybe it wasn't God's voice; perhaps it was my own voice in my head. We then dare to ask our friends, family, and co-workers what they think, or we try to get them to confirm that it was God speaking to you. What is silly about this is that God spoke to you, not your friend, family, or co-worker.

There are even times when we 100% know it's God's voice, but we don't trust him enough to do it or heed his request. We ask others and try to find a way to avoid it. You tell God all kinds of excuses: "You know God that I don't have the money, the talent, the skills. I'm too old. I can't move to this city, state, or country, I don't know anyone."

In our key verse, there is one word that stands out, "IMMEDIATELY." Matthew 4:19-20, "And he said to them, 'Follow me, and I will make you fishers of men.' Immediately, they left their nets and followed him.

If we can sit in a chair without hesitation, why do we hesitate to heed God's voice? By investing in the stock market, cryptocurrency, or other forms of investment, we can potentially increase our wealth. Why can't we invest in consistent time with God? If we can rely on a government (clearly not for the people and corrupt) for the future of our country, then why can't we rely on God, who sits higher than all governments? Who is omnipotent (having unlimited power, able to do anything, all-powerful), omnipresent (present everywhere at the same time), and omniscient (all-knowing/knowing everything).

The closer you get to God, the closer God gets to you, and you will be at a place where your response to God's voice or the Holy Spirit's nudging will be to do it IMMEDIATELY.

WHAT DOES THE BIBLE SAY?

> "[18] While walking by the Sea of Galilee, he saw two brothers, Simon (who is called Peter) and Andrew his brother, casting a net into the sea, for they were fishermen. [19] And he said to them, "Follow me, and I will make you fishers of men."[a] [20] Immediately they left their nets and followed him." (Matthew 4:18-20)

Isaiah 9:1 foretold what would transpire next. The Gospel of Matthew, in chapter 4, explicitly connects this prophecy to Jesus' ministry. Jesus begins his public ministry in Galilee, settling in Capernaum, located by the Sea of Galilee in the territory of Zebulun and Naphtali. Matthew states this was done "so that what was spoken by the prophet Isaiah might be fulfilled."

The prophetic book from the Old Testament, Isaiah 9:1, speaks of this prophecy. The prophecy signifies a shift from darkness and distress to a future filled with light, hope, and glory in a region that had experienced hardship and was known as "Galilee of the Gentiles". Jesus' presence and ministry in this area brought about this transformation and fulfillment.

Jesus begins his public ministry by calling Simon Peter and his brother Andrew to follow Him. The start of the formation of his core group of disciples

Key Words/Phrases

- "**Follow** me, and I will make you fisher of men." (v 19)

- "**Immediately** they left their nets and followed him." (v 20)

- He brought him to Jesus. Jesus looked at him and said, "**You are** Simon the son of John. **You shall be** called Cephas" (which means Peter) (Cephas is Arabic and Peter is Greek and they both mean rock)

Concordance

- **Genesis 12:4:** So, Abram went, as the Lord had told him, and Lot went with him. Abram was seventy-five years old when he departed from Haran.

- **Luke 5:5-6:** And Simon answered, "Master, we toiled all night and took nothing! But at your word I will let down the nets." 6 And when they had done this, they enclosed many fish, and their nets were breaking.

- **Genesis 6 summarized:** Noah obediently built the ark according to the specifications given by God.

- **Exodus 3-12 summarized:** Moses obeyed Gods command to lead the Israelites out of Egypt

WHAT'S THE POINT?

Obedience means responding to God immediately. Half in and half out is disobedience. Following Jesus demonstrates a commitment and willingness to live according to His will. Believers are to put off their old self and put on their new self, the likeness of God.

- Do you trust God enough to move immediately when he speaks to you?

- How can you actively participate in sharing the gospel with others?

KEY SCRIPTURES #2, JOHN 1:40-42

⁴⁰ One of the two who heard John speak and followed Jesus[a] was Andrew, Simon Peter's brother.

⁴¹ He first found his own brother Simon and said to him, "We have found the Messiah" (which means Christ).

⁴² He brought him to Jesus. Jesus looked at him and said, "You are Simon the son of John. You shall be called Cephas" (which means Peter[b]).

LET'S TALK ABOUT IT

We're quick to share good news, like a new job or a financial break-through, or anything else that makes you smile. We immediately (no pun intended) call, text, and reach out to family and friends. We post on social media and are excited to share with anyone who will listen—whether in a community like a church, book club, women's group, men's group, knitting club, golf club, or any other event that brings your family together. These are all needed and intended to celebrate with others. Groups or communities are designed to provide a sense of belonging and opportunities for growth, and they can also offer health benefits and improve your positive outlook on life. As sisters and brothers in Christ, we must unite and support each other, uplift each other, celebrate with each other, and, more importantly, pray for each other and be fishers of men.

WHAT DOES THE BIBLE SAY?

The day before, John the Baptist is standing with two of his disciples, one of whom is Andrew. John the Baptist points out Jesus as he walks by, and John points at Jesus and says, "Look, the Lamb of God." John the Baptist had also used this title after he had baptized Jesus the day before.

Andrew goes to get his brother Simon and brings Simon to meet Jesus with excitement. Andrew had already become a fisher of men before Jesus asked him to follow and do the same. This shows Andrews's willing spirit to point people to Christ Jesus. He knew in his heart that this was the Messiah, and he wanted his brother to meet Jesus as well.

Key Words/Phrases

- "We have found the Messiah" (which means Christ) (v 41)

- He brought him to Jesus. Jesus looked at him and said, "You are Simon the son of John. You shall be called Cephas" (which means Peter) (Cephas is Arabic and Peter is Greek and they both mean rock) (v 42)

- Interpret with Scripture / Comparing other passages about the immediate and powerful desire to share the discovery of Jesus with those closest to you.

- **John 4:28–29:** After Jesus reveals details about her life, the Samaritan woman leaves her water jar and rushes back to her town. Her message is direct: "Come, see a man who told me everything I ever did. Could this be the Messiah?"

- **Mark 5:18–20:** After Jesus heals the man possessed by a «legion» of demons, the man begs to stay with him. However, Jesus commands him, «Go home to your own people and tell them how much the Lord has done for you, and how he has had mercy on you». The man obeys and proclaims his testimony throughout the region of the Decapolis, leading many people to be amazed.

WHAT'S THE POINT?

Sharing the good news, sharing your Christian journey, and being the hands and feet of God. Sharing the love of Jesus and being his disciple in today's world. To be transformed and aim to fulfill His will and purpose for your life.

- How can you help others learn about the Messiah to establish a personal relationship? Remember, your walk, your talk, and your life may be the only Bible some people read.

- Are you willing to be transformed to be used by God?

WEEK 2:
THE CALL OF PETER,
FROM FISHERMAN TO FOLLOWER

THEME

Jesus calls us to leave the familiar and follow Him.

KEY SCRIPTURES, LUKE 5:1–11

> "On one occasion, while the crowd was pressing in on him to hear the word of God, he was standing by the lake of Gennesaret,
>
> [2] and he saw two boats by the lake, but the fishermen had gone out of them and were washing their nets.
>
> [3] Getting into one of the boats, which was Simon's, he asked him to put out a little from the land. And he sat down and taught the people from the boat.

⁴ And when he had finished speaking, he said to Simon, "Put out into the deep and let down your nets for a catch."

⁵ And Simon answered, "Master, we toiled all night and took nothing! But at your word I will let down the nets."

⁶ And when they had done this, they enclosed a large number of fish, and their nets were breaking.

⁷ They signaled to their partners in the other boat to come and help them. And they came and filled both the boats, so that they began to sink.

⁸ But when Simon Peter saw it, he fell down at Jesus' knees, saying, "Depart from me, for I am a sinful man, O Lord."

⁹ For he and all who were with him were astonished at the catch of fish that they had taken,

¹⁰ and so also were James and John, sons of Zebedee, who were partners with Simon. And Jesus said to Simon, "Do not be afraid; from now on you will be catching men."

¹¹ And when they had brought their boats to land, they left everything and followed him."

LET'S TALK ABOUT IT

How many times have you doubted God when he spoke to you, thinking you knew better than God? Or perhaps you wanted something "NOW" and God was taking too long based on your timeline. God is never late, and he is always working on our behalf. He never sleeps nor slumbers, and He knows the beginning and the end. He is alpha and omega. He's omnipotent, knowing all. He's omnipresent, everywhere at the same time, and omniscient, all-knowing. The ultimate goal is for us to let go of old habits and routines, making room for Jesus' new work in our lives and accepting new opportunities for ministry and spiritual growth.

An example of obedience in the Bible is found in Exodus, where God calls Moses to lead the Israelites out of slavery in Egypt. Despite his initial reluctance and doubts about his ability to lead, Moses ultimately obeys God's command and becomes one of the most significant figures in Israelite history.

WHAT DOES THE BIBLE SAY?

This sequence of events follows the baptism of Jesus by John the Baptist, Jesus' temptation in the wilderness by Satan, the rejection of Jesus' message in his hometown of Nazareth, and culminates in Jesus' successful teaching, preaching, and numerous healings in Capernaum, where he gained many believers. One such healing was when Jesus healed Peter's mother-in-law (Luke 4:38-40).

Key Words/Phrases

- "And Simon answered, "Master, we toiled all night and took nothing! **But at your word I will** let down the nets." [6] And when they had done this, they enclosed a large number of fish, and their nets were breaking." (v 5 – 6)

- "But when Simon Peter saw it, he fell down at Jesus' knees, saying, 'Depart from me, for I **am a sinful man**, O Lord." (v 8)

- "And Jesus said to Simon, "Do not be afraid; **from now on** you will be catching men."[a] [11] And when they had brought their boats to land, they left everything and followed him." (v 10-11)

Concordance

- **John 14:15** "If you love me, you will keep my commandments."

- **Deuteronomy 28:1** "And if you faithfully obey the voice of the Lord your God, being careful to do all his commandments that I command you today, the Lord your God will set you high above all the nations of the earth."

- **Acts 5:29** "But Peter and the apostles answered, "We must obey God rather than men."

WHAT'S THE POINT?

Obedience to God and recognizing His divine authority. The supernatural miraculous power of God is throughout the Bible, and it can also apply to your life today. Spiritual transformation is readily available today, along with God's grace and provision. Jesus called the disciples to be fishers of men, not fish. The scripture serves as a model for how Jesus calls people from their everyday lives and failures, transforming them into followers who will carry out His spiritual work.

Jesus calls us to leave the familiar by having complete allegiance to Him, even if it means sacrificing possessions, professions, family, and comfort, because His purposes are more important than our self-preservation or personal dreams. It means placing Christ as your highest treasure and prioritizing His will above all other desires, recognizing that following Him requires a daily, radical abandonment of sin, self-ambition, and anything else that stands in the way of total devotion to Him.

- To what extent do you recognize and submit to Jesus' authority?

- Is there anything in your life that you are having a hard time releasing to Jesus?

- Are you an active follower of Jesus or an admirer of Jesus?

- Are you seeking your identity and purpose in things or people rather than in Jesus?

WEEK 3:
THE GROWTH OF PETER,
FROM BOLDNESS TO BROKENNESS

THEME

God shapes us through both triumphs and failures.

KEY SCRIPTURE #1, MATTHEW 14: 22-33

"[22] Immediately he made the disciples get into the boat and go before him to the other side, while he dismissed the crowds.

[23] And after he had dismissed the crowds, he went up on the mountain by himself to pray. When evening came, he was there alone,

[24] but the boat by this time was a long way[a] from the land,[b] beaten by the waves, for the wind was against them.

[25] And in the fourth watch of the night[c] he came to them, walking on the sea.

²⁶ But when the disciples saw him walking on the sea, they were terrified, and said, "It is a ghost!" and they cried out in fear.

²⁷ But immediately Jesus spoke to them, saying, "Take heart; it is I. Do not be afraid."

²⁸ And Peter answered him, "Lord, if it is you, command me to come to you on the water."

²⁹ He said, "Come." So Peter got out of the boat and walked on the water and came to Jesus.

³⁰ But when he saw the wind,[d] he was afraid, and beginning to sink he cried out, "Lord, save me."

³¹ Jesus immediately reached out his hand and took hold of him, saying to him, "O you of little faith, why did you doubt?"

³² And when they got into the boat, the wind ceased.

³³ And those in the boat worshiped him, saying, "Truly you are the Son of God."

Let's Talk About It

Imagine a young woman named Jennifer, a committed believer who leads worship at her church. One Sunday, as she sings, she feels the presence of God so strongly that she declares with conviction, "Jesus, You're everything I'll ever need!" This becomes her own version of Peter's confession, "You are the Christ, the Son of the living God." But that same week, when a co-worker mocks her faith, she stays silent, afraid of being ridiculed, much like Peter's denial by the fire. Later, in prayer, she feels God inviting her to step out in faith and apply for a missions trip she has been afraid to join, echoing Peter stepping onto the water.

At first, Jennifer feels bold and unstoppable. Yet when challenges arise such as deadlines, doubt, and fear of failure, she begins to sink. Like Peter, she cries out, and Jesus immediately reaches for her hand. Through these moments of courage and collapse, confession and correction, Jennifer learns what Peter discovered: real faith is not proven by never falling but by always reaching back for Christ.

What does the Bible say?

This follows the feeding of the 5,000. Jesus sends His disciples ahead, while He goes to pray. The storm reveals their fear and need for trust.

Key Words/Phrases

- "Take heart; it is I. **Do not be afraid.**" (v. 27)

- "Come." (v. 29)

- "Lord, save me!" (v. 30)

- "O ye of little faith, why did you doubt?" (v. 31)

Concordance

- **Isaiah 41:10** "fear not, for I am with you; be not dismayed, for I am your God; I will strengthen you, I will help you, I will uphold you with my righteous right hand.

- **Psalm 46:1–3** "God is our refuge and strength, a very present[b] help in trouble. 2 Therefore we will not fear though the earth give way, though the mountains be moved into the heart of the sea, 3 though its waters roar and foam, though the mountains tremble at its swelling."

- **Psalm 34:4** ""I sought the Lord, and he answered me and delivered me from all my fears."

WHAT'S THE POINT?

Faith means keeping our eyes on Jesus, not on the storms around us. When fear overtakes us, Jesus is still near to save.

- Where is Jesus calling you to step out in faith?

- Do you trust Him when the storms of life rise?

- When have you felt your faith begin to "sink" under the weight of fear or doubt?

- Where do you sense Jesus still reaching out His hand to you today?

- How can you encourage others to keep their eyes on Jesus?

KEY SCRIPTURE #2, MATTHEW 16:13–23

"13 Now when Jesus came into the district of Caesarea Philippi, he asked his disciples, "Who do people say that the Son of Man is?"

14 And they said, "Some say John the Baptist, others say Elijah, and others Jeremiah or one of the prophets."

15 He said to them, "But who do you say that I am?"

16 Simon Peter replied, "You are the Christ, the Son of the living God."

17 And Jesus answered him, "Blessed are you, Simon Bar-Jonah! For flesh and blood has not revealed this to you, but my Father who is in heaven.

18 And I tell you, you are Peter, and on this rock[a] I will build my church, and the gates of hell[b] shall not prevail against it.

19 I will give you the keys of the kingdom of heaven, and whatever you bind on earth shall be bound in heaven, and whatever you loose on earth shall be loosed[c] in heaven."

[20] Then he strictly charged the disciples to tell no one that he was the Christ.

[21] From that time Jesus began to show his disciples that he must go to Jerusalem and suffer many things from the elders and chief priests and scribes, and be killed, and on the third day be raised.

[22] And Peter took him aside and began to rebuke him, saying, "Far be it from you, Lord![d] This shall never happen to you."

[23] But he turned and said to Peter, "Get behind me, Satan! You are a hindrance[e] to me. For you are not setting your mind on the things of God, but on the things of man."

LET'S TALK ABOUT IT

This follows the interactions Jesus has with the Pharisees and Sadducees and how they demanded Jesus show them a sign from heaven to prove his authority. Jesus refers to the "sign of Jonah" as the only sign he will give this generation, a reference to Jonah spending three days in the belly of the great fish to his own time spent in the tomb before his resurrection. Jesus warns the disciples to beware of the leaven of the Pharisees and Sadducees. The disciples thought Jesus was speaking of physical bread. (5 loaves feeding 5,000) Jesus was using figurative language to reference the leaven of bread as the teaching of the Pharisees and Sadducees, and for the disciples to be cautious of their teaching.

WHAT DOES THE BIBLE SAY?

Key Words/Phrases

- [15] He said to them, "But who do you say that I am?" [16] Simon Peter replied, "You are the Christ, the Son of the living God." [17] And Jesus answered him, "Blessed are you, Simon Bar-Jonah! For **flesh and blood has not revealed this to you, but my Father who is in heaven.**" (v. 15 -17)

- "and on this rock[a] I **will build my church**" (v 18)

- "[19] I will give you **the keys of the kingdom of heaven,** and whatever you bind on earth shall be bound in heaven, and whatever you loose on earth shall be loosed[c] in heaven." (v 19)

- "[22] And Peter took him aside and began to rebuke him, saying, "Far be it from you, Lord![d] This shall never happen to you." [23] But he turned and said to Peter, **"Get behind me, Satan!** You are a hindrance[e] to me. For you are not setting your mind on the things of God, but on the things of man." (v. 22-23)

Concordance

- **Matthew 12:40** "[40] For just as Jonah was three days and three nights in the belly of the great fish, so will the Son of Man be three days and three nights in the heart of the earth.

- **John 2:19-22** "[9] Jesus answered them, "Destroy this temple, and in three days I will raise it up." [20] The Jews then said, "It has taken forty-six years to build this temple,[a] and will you raise it up in three days?" [21] But he was speaking about the temple of his body. [22] When therefore he was raised from the dead, his disciples remembered that he had said this, and they believed the Scripture and the word that Jesus had spoken."

WHAT'S THE POINT?

Jesus deliberately took his disciples to Caesarea Philippi which was a city built literally on a rock, to ask, "Who do people say that the Son of Man is?" and "Who do you say that I am?". The pagan and idolatrous setting of the city was key to the significance of the question and the revelation that followed. Ancient people believed a deep cave in this area to be a gateway to the underworld, or Hades. When Peter declared Jesus to be the Messiah, Jesus responded, "And I tell you, you are Peter, and on this rock (keep in mind they were in a city that was built on a rock) I will build my church, and the gates of hell shall not prevail against it" (Matthew 16:18). By referencing the pagan gates of Hades in their very presence, Jesus was making a powerful declaration that his church would overcome the spiritual forces of evil represented by that location.

- Jesus asked, "But who do you say that I am?" How would you respond to this question in your own words? Has your understanding of Jesus evolved?

- Jesus called Peter "Satan" when Peter was not setting his mind on the things of God, but rather on the things of man, and he tried to dissuade Him from suffering and death. How can well-meaning Christians occasionally become stumbling blocks to God's purposes?

KEY SCRIPTURE #3, LUKE 22:54–62

"⁵⁴ Then they seized him and led him away, bringing him into the high priest's house, and Peter was following at a distance.

⁵⁵ And when they had kindled a fire in the middle of the courtyard and sat down together, Peter sat down among them.

⁵⁶ Then a servant girl, seeing him as he sat in the light and looking closely at him, said, "This man also was with him."

⁵⁷ But he denied it, saying, "Woman, I do not know him."

⁵⁸ And a little later someone else saw him and said, "You also are one of them." But Peter said, "Man, I am not."

⁵⁹ And after an interval of about an hour still another insisted, saying, "Certainly this man also was with him, for he too is a Galilean."

⁶⁰ But Peter said, "Man, I do not know what you are talking about." And immediately, while he was still speaking, the rooster crowed.

> *⁶¹ And the Lord turned and looked at Peter. And Peter remembered the saying of the Lord, how he had said to him, "Before the rooster crows today, you will deny me three times."*

> *⁶² And he went out and wept bitterly."*

LET'S TALK ABOUT IT

As a Christian who believes in the power of prayer, the power of fellowship, the power of God's word, and the power of attending church to worship God and be fed the word of God. There may be times when you get a text that reads: _Pray for Mary. It's bad._ Or you open the mail to bills that you don't have the funds to pay. Your child may be involved with the wrong crowd, and you have just been laid off.

How do you regain that faith? How do you focus on the hand of Jesus reaching for you instead of the wind and waves blowing against you? You were once the individual that people came to for prayer; however, now your prayers feel as if they aren't getting through.

You start to doubt yourself and doubt God.

Someone may ask you to pray for them at work, and you say, "I'm too busy."

A few days later someone may ask to attend church with you and you say, "I'm too busy to attend church right now."

Later in the week you are invited to attend bible study, you decline and say, "I'm too busy."

And the siren starts to go off in your head.

It isn't the sound of judgment but of realization — piercing, unignorable, cutting straight through the noise in your head. The truth of yourself starts to press hard in your mind, not the confident worship leader, not the one who prayers for other — just a person afraid of losing God.

You're at home after work and the Pastor calls and says "Come back when you're ready. Grace still waits."

You read the message a few times and somewhere in silence between evening and sunrise, you began to understand — faith was never about standing tall on the water. It was about sinking, reaching out, and finding that the hand still waits, even when you've already let go.

Reflection

Like Peter and the storm, you realize that storms have a way of testing whether faith is built on calm waters or on the One who commands them.

In Matthew 14, Peter's confidence faltered when the wind rose. In Matthew 16, his insight into who Jesus was didn't protect him from misunderstanding what Jesus came to do. And in Luke 22, his courage failed when fear closed in.

We have all experienced the pattern — the rise of faith, the misunderstanding of its strength, and the breaking point that reveals both weakness and grace.

Failure isn't the end of faith. In both stories, grace reaches back — not to erase the denial, but to redeem the heart that made it.

This follows Jesus' arrest after being betrayed by Judas Iscariot, who was paid thirty pieces of silver, and Peter's subsequent pursuit of the arresting party to the high priest's house.

WHAT DOES THE BIBLE SAY?

Key Words/Phrases

- "and immediately, while he was still speaking, the rooster crowed. [61] And the Lord turned and looked at Peter. And **Peter remembered the saying of the Lord,** how he had said to him, "Before the rooster crows today, you will deny me three times." [62] And he went out and wept bitterly." (v 60-62)

Concordance

- **Titus 1:16** "[16] They profess to know God, but they deny him by their works. They are detestable, disobedient, unfit for any good work."

- **Matthew 10:33** "[33] but whoever denies me before men, I also will deny before my Father who is in heaven."

- **2 Timothy 2:12** "If we endure, we will also reign with him; if we deny him, he also will deny us."

WHAT'S THE POINT?

- This passage illustrates Peter's denial of Jesus three times, as Jesus had predicted, before the rooster crowed three times. The passage emphasizes his extreme grief and sadness.

- (This does not reference this scripture however, it does speak to the three times of denial) Jesus asked Peter three times if he loved him in John 21:15-17, after his resurrection. This threefold questioning served to restore Peter after his three denials of Jesus and to commission him as a leader to "feed my sheep". The repetition was a deliberate act of grace, allowing Peter to affirm his love for Christ three times, matching his earlier denials and confirming his renewed commitment to his ministry.

- Do you follow Jesus "at a distance"? How can you get closer to Jesus?

- Peter's denial didn't end his story — he was later restored by Jesus (John 21:15–19). How can that restoration shape how we see our own failures?

- How can we be encouraged by the fact that God wasn't finished with Peter after his failure, and He isn't finished with you either?

WEEK 4:
THE RESTORATION OF PETER, FROM FAILURE TO FORGIVENESS

Theme

Jesus restores us and recommissions us for service.

Key Scripture #1, John 21:15-19

"When they had finished breakfast, Jesus said to Simon Peter, "Simon, son of John, do you love me more than these?" He said to him, "Yes, Lord; you know that I love you." He said to him, "Feed my lambs."

[16] He said to him a second time, "Simon, son of John, do you love me?" He said to him, "Yes, Lord; you know that I love you." He said to him, "Tend my sheep."

[17] He said to him the third time, "Simon, son of John, do you love me?" Peter was grieved because he said to him the third time, "Do you love me?" and he said to him, "Lord, you know

everything; you know that I love you." Jesus said to him, "Feed my sheep.

[18] Truly, truly, I say to you, when you were young, you used to dress yourself and walk wherever you wanted, but when you are old, you will stretch out your hands, and another will dress you and carry you where you do not want to go."

[19] (This he said to show by what kind of death he was to glorify God.) And after saying this he said to him, "Follow me."

LET'S TALK ABOUT IT

Before the crucifixion of Jesus, Peter denied Jesus three times before the rooster crowed, he immediately realized he had done exactly as Jesus had predicted. He "wept bitterly." Now, after the resurrection, Jesus questioned Peter three times about whether he loved Him, while at the same time, Jesus was giving instructions on feeding His lambs, tending His sheep, and feeding His Sheep.

There are many examples in life when someone was hurt, relations damaged, loved ones who lost their lives, but the hurt person or injured person or survivors of the deceased forgave the person(s) who caused the pain.

Real-life example - A mother forgiving her son's murderer: In 1993, Mary Johnson's son was murdered by a young man named Oshea Israel. After Israel was sentenced to prison, Johnson felt a strong urge to forgive him. They later met and developed a close bond. When Israel was released, she helped him transition back to the neighborhood, where he lived next door to her. Johnson stated, **"unforgiveness is like cancer. It will eat you from the inside out."**

A Religious parable: Joseph forgiving his brothers. After his brothers sold him into slavery out of jealousy, Joseph rose to a position of great power in Egypt. When his brothers later came to him for food during a famine, they did not recognize him. Joseph eventually revealed his identity but did not seek revenge. Instead, he forgave them, explaining that God used their evil actions for a greater.

There is a saying, "anger is like holding a hot coal," which illustrates that clinging to anger primarily harms oneself, not the intended target, as one is the one who gets burned by it.

WHY ANGER BLOCKS BLESSINGS

- **Creates a barrier:** Bitterness and anger build invisible walls between you and God, preventing you from walking in the fullness of His grace and love.

- **Prevents trust:** Holding onto anger makes it difficult to trust God's perfect timing and justice, weighing you down instead of allowing for freedom.

- **Distracts from God's work:** Energy focused on anger and resentment is energy not spent on the good things God is working on in your life.

- **Hindrance to God's forgiveness:** The Bible teaches that forgiveness from God is contingent on our forgiveness of others, as seen in Matthew 6:14-15.

How to Unlock Blessings

Forgive and release:

- **Choose to forgive** those who have wronged you, which doesn't mean forgetting or excusing their behavior but rather releasing the hold they have in your heart.

- **Trust God's justice:** Trust that God sees everything and will fight your battles, bringing justice in His perfect timing.

- **Let go:** Release the burdens of revenge and bitterness to open yourself to the peace and joy God desires for you.

- **Seek His presence:** Make space for God's peace to fill your life by letting go of the emotional weight of anger and bitterness.

Why does the Bible say?

Before this scripture, Jesus' disciples, including Peter, were fishing after his resurrection when Jesus appeared on the shore and guided them to a massive catch of fish, which led them to recognize him and prepare a meal. This event served as a precursor to Jesus' restoration of Peter, who had previously denied knowing Jesus three times during his trial, an act that Jesus addressed by asking Peter three times if he loved him.

Key Words/Phrases

- "Simon, son of John, d**o you love me more than these**?.. "Feed my lambs.... "Simon, son of John, do you love me?"... "Tend my sheep.".. "Simon, son of John, do you love me?" ... "Feed my sheep" (v 15 - 17)

- **"Follow me."** (v 19)

Concordance

- **Ephesians 4:32** "Be kind to one another, tenderhearted, forgiving one another, as God in Christ forgave you."

- **Matthew 6:14** "For if you forgive others their trespasses, your heavenly Father will also forgive you,"

- **Luke 6:37** "Judge not, and you will not be judged; condemn not, and you will not be condemned; forgive, and you will be forgiven;"

- **Matthew 18:21-22** "Then Peter came up and said to him, "Lord, how often will my brother sin against me, and I forgive him? As many as seven times?" [22] Jesus said to him, "I do not say to you seven times, but seventy-seven times."

- **Matthew 6:15** "but if you do not forgive others their trespasses, neither will your Father forgive your trespasses."

- **Hebrews 8:12** "For I will be merciful toward their iniquities, and I will remember their sins no more."

- **Proverbs 17:9** "Whoever covers an offense seeks love, but he who repeats a matter separates close friends.

WHAT'S THE POINT?

The main point of John 21:15-19 is Jesus' threefold restoration of Peter through a series of questions asking if he loves Jesus, which confirms his love and commissions him to a ministry of tending God's people. Three times Peter denied Jesus before the crucifixion and three times Jesus questions Peters love for him after resurrection. The passage highlights that love for Christ is demonstrated through action and service, and that past failures do not disqualify a person from being used by God.

- What are the "these" in your life—the things you put before God? Is it your career, family, possessions, or personal ambitions?

- Do you still carry guilt from past failures, or have you accepted Christ's full forgiveness and restoration, just as Peter did?

- What is your commission from Jesus? In what ways are you called to feed and care for his people?

- What is the difference between "feeding" (teaching) and "tending" (caring) for others? Am I doing both, or am I focused on only one aspect of ministry?

- Am I ministering to God's people as his sheep, not my own? Am I focused on his flock›s growth and nourishment, or on building my own kingdom?

After the conversation, Jesus' final command is "Follow me." He calls us to a life of discipleship that often requires surrendering our own plans and desires. How can you follow Jesus closer tomorrow than you do today?

KEY SCRIPTURE #2, ACTS 2:14-41

Peter's Sermon at Pentecost

"But Peter, standing with the eleven, lifted up his voice and addressed them: "Men of Judea and all who dwell in Jerusalem, let this be known to you, and give ear to my words.

¹⁵ For these people are not drunk, as you suppose, since it is only the third hour of the day.[a]

¹⁶ But this is what was uttered through the prophet Joel:

¹⁷ "'And in the last days it shall be, God declares, that I will pour out my Spirit on all flesh, and your sons and your daughters shall prophesy, and your young men shall see visions, and your old men shall dream dreams;

¹⁸ even on my male servants and female servants in those days I will pour out my Spirit, and they shall prophesy.

¹⁹ And I will show wonders in the heavens above and signs on the earth below, blood, and fire, and vapor of smoke;

[20] *the sun shall be turned to darkness and the moon to blood, before the day of the Lord comes, the great and magnificent day.*

[21] *And it shall come to pass that everyone who calls upon the name of the Lord shall be saved.'*

[22] *"Men of Israel, hear these words: Jesus of Nazareth, a man attested to you by God with mighty works and wonders and signs that God did through him in your midst, as you yourselves know—*

[23] *this Jesus,[b] delivered up according to the definite plan and foreknowledge of God, you crucified and killed by the hands of lawless men.*

[24] *God raised him up, loosing the pangs of death, because it was not possible for him to be held by it.*

[25] *For David says concerning him, "'I saw the Lord always before me, for he is at my right hand that I may not be shaken;*

[26] *therefore my heart was glad, and my tongue rejoiced; my flesh also will dwell in hope.*

²⁷ For you will not abandon my soul to Hades, or let your Holy One see corruption.

²⁸ You have made known to me the paths of life; you will make me full of gladness with your presence.'

²⁹ "Brothers, I may say to you with confidence about the patriarch David that he both died and was buried, and his tomb is with us to this day.

³⁰ Being therefore a prophet, and knowing that God had sworn with an oath to him that he would set one of his descendants on his throne,

³¹ he foresaw and spoke about the resurrection of the Christ, that he was not abandoned to Hades, nor did his flesh see corruption.

³² This Jesus God raised up, and of that we all are witnesses.

³³ Being therefore exalted at the right hand of God, and having received from the Father the promise of the Holy Spirit, he has poured out this that you yourselves are seeing and hearing.

34 For David did not ascend into the heavens, but he himself says, "'The Lord said to my Lord, "Sit at my right hand,

35 until I make your enemies your footstool."'

36 Let all the house of Israel therefore know for certain that God has made him both Lord and Christ, this Jesus whom you crucified."

37 Now when they heard this they were cut to the heart, and said to Peter and the rest of the apostles, "Brothers, what shall we do?"

38 And Peter said to them, "Repent and be baptized every one of you in the name of Jesus Christ for the forgiveness of your sins, and you will receive the gift of the Holy Spirit.

39 For the promise is for you and for your children and for all who are far off, everyone whom the Lord our God calls to himself."

40 And with many other words he bore witness and continued to exhort them, saying, "Save yourselves from this crooked generation."

> ⁴¹ *So those who received his word were baptized, and there were added that day about three thousand souls.*

Let's Talk About It

Michael had always been quiet about his faith. He believed in Jesus, but he rarely spoke up in public. One evening, his church hosted an open-air community event. As the worship team finished, the microphone was passed to anyone who wanted to share a word. Michael felt a stirring in his heart but hesitated. Then, with trembling hands, he stood up and began to speak about how God had changed his life. His voice was unsure at first, but as he continued, conviction filled his words. He spoke about forgiveness, purpose, and the power of Jesus to transform lives.

Much like Peter on the day of Pentecost in Acts 2:14–41, Michael discovered that the Holy Spirit gives courage and clarity when we step forward in obedience. People listened, some with tears in their eyes, and several came forward for prayer. That night, Michael learned that boldness is not about confidence in ourselves but confidence in the message of Christ. When the Spirit speaks through us, ordinary voices become instruments of extraordinary grace.

WHAT DOES THE BIBLE SAY?

Before the passage Acts 2:14-41, the disciples received the Holy Spirit at Pentecost, causing them to speak in other tongues and leading to a crowd's confusion. In response, Peter, accompanied by the other apostles, delivered his sermon from verses 14-41, explaining the event by quoting the prophet Joel, rebuking the accusation of drunkenness, and calling the crowd to repent and be baptized in Jesus' name.

The Prophet Joel live about 400 years before the birth of Jesus. The book of Joel is about 4 chapters long and the main message of the Book of Joel is that of salvation amid judgment, centered on the concept of the "Day of the Lord." God's people are called to repent in the face of impending judgment, symbolized by a devastating locust plague. The prophet assures that after the judgment and repentance, God will pour out His Spirit on all people, bringing deliverance and restoration. Pour out His Spirt, which takes us to Acts 2:14-41.

The Key Words/Phrases

- "These people are not drunk, as you suppose. It's only nine in the morning!" (v 15)

- 'In the last days, God says, I will pour out my Spirit on all people" (v 17)

- "And everyone who calls on the name of the Lord will be saved." (v 21)

- "God has raised this Jesus to life, and we are all witnesses of it. ^{33} Exalted to the right hand of God, he has received from the Father the promised Holy Spirit and has poured out what you now see and hear." (v 32-33)

- "Those who accepted his message were baptized, and about three thousand were added to their number that day." (v 41)

Concordance

- **Acts 3:19** "Repent, then, and turn to God, so that your sins may be wiped out."

What's the Point?

This was Peter's first sermon, the Day of Pentecost, as recorded in Acts 2. At this event, after receiving the Holy Spirit, Peter addressed the crowd in Jerusalem, explaining the miraculous events of Jesus how Jesus is the promised Messiah, whose life, death, and resurrection fulfill ancient prophecies. The sermon culminates in a powerful call to repentance and baptism, offering the forgiveness of sins and the gift of the Holy Spirit to all who believe in Jesus. This sermon marked the birth of the Christian church and resulted in over 3,000 new believers being baptized.

- How does Peter's transformation from a fearful denial of Jesus to a bold preacher illustrate the power of the Holy Spirit, and how does this story inspire you to rely on the Spirit in your own life?

- Reflect on your own weaknesses, fears, or areas where you feel inadequate. How can the Holy Spirit empower you to overcome these limitations to do what God intends?

- The early believers devoted themselves to teaching, fellowship, the breaking of bread, prayer, and were characterized by generosity and unity. How does this model of community challenge your own Christian community or individual practices?

- How can you contribute to a more vibrant, welcoming, and generous Christian community in your church or small group, reflecting the spirit of Acts?

- Prayer/takeaway: Pray for boldness and clarity to share the message of Jesus Christ, and seek ways to be involved in bringing others to faith.

WEEK 5:
THE LEGACY OF PETER, FROM DISCIPLE TO MARTYR

THEME

A faithful life leaves a lasting legacy.

KEY SCRIPTURE #1, ACTS 10:34–48

Hear the Good News

> "*So Peter opened his mouth and said: "Truly I understand that God shows no partiality,*
>
> *35 but in every nation anyone who fears him and does what is right is acceptable to him.*
>
> *36 As for the word that he sent to Israel, preaching good news of peace through Jesus Christ (he is Lord of all),*
>
> *37 you yourselves know what happened throughout all Judea, beginning from Galilee after the baptism that John proclaimed:*

³⁸ how God anointed Jesus of Nazareth with the Holy Spirit and with power. He went about doing good and healing all who were oppressed by the devil, for God was with him.

³⁹ And we are witnesses of all that he did both in the country of the Jews and in Jerusalem. They put him to death by hanging him on a tree,

⁴⁰ but God raised him on the third day and made him to appear,

⁴¹ not to all the people but to us who had been chosen by God as witnesses, who ate and drank with him after he rose from the dead.

⁴² And he commanded us to preach to the people and to testify that he is the one appointed by God to be judge of the living and the dead.

⁴³ To him all the prophets bear witness that everyone who believes in him receives forgiveness of sins through his name."

The Holy Spirit Falls on the Gentiles

⁴⁴ While Peter was still saying these things, the Holy Spirit fell on all who heard the word.

⁴⁵ And the believers from among the circumcised who had come with Peter were amazed, because the gift of the Holy Spirit was poured out even on the Gentiles.

⁴⁶ For they were hearing them speaking in tongues and extolling God. Then Peter declared,

⁴⁷ "Can anyone withhold water for baptizing these people, who have received the Holy Spirit just as we have?"

⁴⁸ And he commanded them to be baptized in the name of Jesus Christ. Then they asked him to remain for some days."

LET'S TALK ABOUT IT

In Acts 10:34–48, Peter stands before Cornelius and his household and declares that God shows no partiality, welcoming all who believe in Jesus Christ. This passage invites you to see how wide God's mercy truly is. You may have grown up believing that faith belonged to a certain group or that God favored people who looked, prayed, or lived like you. Yet in this story, the Holy Spirit falls on everyone in the room, including those Peter once thought were outsiders.

You are reminded that God's presence cannot be confined by background, culture, or custom. The same Spirit that transformed Peter is working in you to break down barriers of bias, fear, and exclusion. When you open your heart to people who are different from you—welcoming them into friendship, conversation, and worship—you become part of the same miracle that took place in Cornelius's house. The Spirit still moves wherever hearts are ready to receive.

WHAT DOES THE BIBLE SAY?

Key Words/Phrases

1. **"God shows no partiality"** (v. 34)

   – The central declaration of divine impartiality and inclusivity.

2. **"In every nation anyone who fears Him and does what is right is acceptable to Him"** (v. 35)

   – Highlights the universality of the gospel.

3. **"The good news of peace through Jesus Christ—He is Lord of all"** (v. 36)

   – Announces the message and scope of Christ's lordship.

4. **"God anointed Jesus of Nazareth with the Holy Spirit and with power"** (v. 38)

   – Underscores Jesus' divine commissioning and ministry.

5. **"He went about doing good and healing all who were oppressed by the devil"** (v. 38)

   – Summarizes the nature of Christ's earthly work.

6. **"We are witnesses of all that He did"** (v. 39)

   – Affirms apostolic testimony as the foundation of faith.

7. **"They put Him to death by hanging Him on a tree"** (v. 39)

   – Proclaims the crucifixion as the means of redemption.

8. **"God raised Him on the third day"** (v. 40)

   – Declares the resurrection as God's vindication of Jesus.

9. **"He commanded us to preach... that He is the one ordained by God to be Judge of the living and the dead"** (v. 42)

   – Reveals the universal authority of Christ.

10. **"Everyone who believes in Him receives forgiveness of sins through His name"** (v. 43)

    – The gospel's invitation to all humanity.

11. **"The Holy Spirit fell upon all who heard the word"** (v. 44)

    – Marks the Gentile Pentecost—God's inclusive outpouring.

12. **"They were speaking in tongues and extolling God"** (v. 46)

    – Evidence of the Spirit's presence and unity of faith.

13. **"Can anyone withhold water for baptizing these people?"** (v. 47)

    – Invitation to baptism as confirmation of belonging.

14. **"They have received the Holy Spirit just as we have"** (v. 47)

– Affirmation of equality in salvation and Spirit.

WHAT'S THE POINT?

God's grace is impartial, His Spirit is inclusive, and His salvation is available to all who believe.

Acts 10:34–48 proclaims the breaking of every boundary—religious, ethnic, and cultural—through the power of the risen Christ.

KEY SCRIPTURE #2, 1 PETER 1:3-9 BORN AGAIN TO A LIVING HOPE

> [3] *Blessed be the God and Father of our Lord Jesus Christ! According to his great mercy, he has caused us to be born again to a living hope through the resurrection of Jesus Christ from the dead,*

> [4] *to an inheritance that is imperishable, undefiled, and unfading, kept in heaven for you,*

> [5] *who by God's power are being guarded through faith for a salvation ready to be revealed in the last time.*

> [6] *In this you rejoice, though now for a little while, if necessary, you have been grieved by various trials,*

> [7] *so that the tested genuineness of your faith— more precious than gold that perishes though it is tested by fire—may be found to result in praise and glory and honor at the revelation of Jesus Christ.*

> [8] *Though you have not seen him, you love him. Though you do not now see him, you believe in him and rejoice with joy that is inexpressible and filled with glory,*

⁹*obtaining the outcome of your faith, the salvation of your souls."*

LET'S TALK ABOUT IT

In 1 Peter 1:3–9, you are reminded that your faith is anchored in a living hope, not a fragile optimism. Because Jesus rose from the dead, your future is not uncertain; it is secure. You have an inheritance that can never perish, spoil, or fade, and it is being kept in heaven for you. Even when life feels heavy with trials, your faith is being refined like gold in the fire. The testing of your faith is not meant to destroy you but to prove the genuineness of what God has placed inside you.

You may not see Christ with your physical eyes, but you love Him. You trust Him even in seasons when you cannot feel Him. Every tear you shed and every prayer whispered through pain becomes part of your worship. Through it all, God is shaping you into a person of enduring faith. The joy that comes from believing in Jesus is deeper than emotion; it is the quiet confidence that no loss, no suffering, and no darkness can erase the salvation waiting for you in Him.

WHAT DOES THE BIBLE SAY?

The context of this scripture is that the resurrection of Jesus provides hope and a guaranteed inheritance, kept safe in heaven that can not be tarnished, destroyed or lost.

Key Words/Phrases

- "he has caused us to be born again to a living hope through the resurrection of Jesus Christ from the dead." (v 3)

- "Though you have not seen him, you love him. Though you do not now see him, you believe in him and rejoice with joy" (v 8)

Concordance

- **John 3:16-17** "For God so loved the world,[a] that he gave his only Son, that whoever believes in him should not perish but have eternal life. [17] For God did not send his Son into the world to condemn the world, but in order that the world might be saved through him."

- **Titus 1:2** "in hope of eternal life, which God, who never lies, promised before the ages began"

- **Romans 15:13** "May the God of hope fill you with all joy and peace in believing, so that by the power of the Holy Spirit you may abound in hope."

WHAT'S THE POINT?

The main point of 1 Peter 1:3-9 is that believers have a secure, living hope in God's unfading, never-ending inheritance, which allows them to find joy and endure suffering, as their faith's genuineness is being tested and proven to bring praise and glory to Jesus Christ. This hope is rooted in Christ's resurrection and sustained by God's power through faith, offering assurance and confidence even amidst trials

- What is your source of hope: What are the specific things you currently put your hope in daily (e.g., work, relationships, success, personal abilities)? Do these contrast with the "living hope" described in the passage?

- Has your faith ever been tested? Are you allowing God to test and refine your faith through trials, similar to how fire refines gold? What is God refining in you right now?

- What specific changes you can make to live with greater perseverance and humility, ensuring your faith is a testimony of God's power to change lives.

KEY SCRIPTURE #3, 2 PETER 1:12-15

"Therefore, I intend always to remind you of these qualities, though you know them and are established in the truth that you have.

[13] I think it right, as long as I am in this body,[a] to stir you up by way of reminder,

[14] since I know that the putting off of my body will be soon, as our Lord Jesus Christ made clear to me.

[15] And I will make every effort so that after my departure you may be able at any time to recall these things."

LET'S TALK ABOUT IT

At your church, imagine a small Bible study that meets every Wednesday evening. Over time, the group has grown close, sharing meals, prayers, and honest conversations about faith. One evening, the leader opens with 2 Peter 1:12–15 and says, "I know we've talked about these truths many times before, but I want to remind you of them again." Some members nod, realizing how easily life's demands have pulled their attention away from prayer, gratitude, and Scripture. The discussion becomes a gentle call to return to the basics—trusting God daily, loving one another, and staying grounded in the promises they already know.

In the weeks that follow, each person begins to see the value of repetition and remembrance. The group starts texting one another Scripture verses throughout the week, encouraging each other to stay focused. A newer believer shares how these reminders kept her steady through a difficult diagnosis, while an older member says he finally understands why Peter wanted believers to remember even what they already knew. The study ends with renewed purpose: to live and teach in such a way that when others look back, they will remember faith not as a theory, but as a life well lived in Christ.

WHAT DOES THE BIBLE SAY?

Before 2 Peter 1:12–15, the preceding verses (2 Peter 1:3–11) described how believers are equipped with divine power for a godly life and urged them to diligently pursue spiritual growth by adding various virtues/Christian qualities to their faith.

Key Words/Phrases

- "to remind you" (v 12)

- "to stir you" (v13)

- "since I know that the putting off of my body will be soon, as our Lord Jesus Christ made clear to me." (v14)

- "And I will make every effort so that after my departure you may be able at any time to recall these things." (v15)

Concordance

- **Galatians 5:22-23** " But the fruit of the Spirit is love, joy, peace, patience, kindness, goodness, faithfulness, [23] gentleness, self-control; against such things there is no law."

- **1 Corinthians 13:13** "So now faith, hope, and love abide, these three; but the greatest of these is love."

- **Philippians 4:8** "Finally, brothers, whatever is true, whatever is honorable, whatever is just, whatever is pure, whatever is lovely, whatever is commendable, if there is any excellence, if there is anything worthy of praise, think about these things."

WHAT'S THE POINT?

The main point was for Peter to explain his motivation for writing due to his death being near. He wanted to serve as a constant reminder of the truths for his readers. Peter's intention in these verses is to stir up his readers' spiritual growth and to ensure they can recall these teachings even after he is gone. He sees his letter as a "last will and testament".

- How often do you engage with God's Word? How can you be more consistent in reading, studying and reflecting on Scripture? As Peter stated, it is necessary to keep spiritual truth alive.

- Are you living out the truth, or just hearing it? How can you become a doer more often and how can your daily actions and choices demonstrate your understanding and belief in God's teachings?

- What steps can you take to improve your spiritual clarity and commitment? Think about specific actions you can take, such as attending Bible study, engaging in discussions with other believers, or prioritizing time for prayer and scripture, to grow spiritually and stay connected to God's truth.

WEEK 6:
PETER AND THE CHURCH,
THE ROCK ON WHICH CHRIST BUILDS

THEME

Christ builds His church through transformed people who stand firm in faith.

KEY SCRIPTURES

Matthew 16:13–19; Acts 2:42–47; 1 Peter 2:4–10

LET'S TALK ABOUT IT

The church today faces cultural shifts, changing values, and new challenges to its faith. Yet, like Peter, believers are called to be living stones built on Christ, the cornerstone. Just as Peter once stumbled and was restored, we are called to bring our brokenness before God so that He may use us to strengthen others. The early church was not built on buildings or programs but on faith, fellowship, and the power of the Holy Spirit.

WHAT DOES THE BIBLE SAY?

In Matthew 16, Jesus declares that Peter's confession, 'You are the Christ, the Son of the Living God', would be the foundation upon which His Church is built. In Acts 2, the same Peter preaches boldly, and the community of believers devotes themselves to teaching, fellowship, breaking of bread, and prayer. In 1 Peter 2, he reminds us that believers are a chosen people, a royal priesthood, called to proclaim God's excellence.

Key Words/Phrases

- **On this rock** I will build my church." (Matthew 16:18)

- "They **devoted themselves** to the apostles' teaching and to fellowship." (Acts 2:42)

- "You also, like living stones, **are being built** into a spiritual house." (1 Peter 2:5)

Concordance

- Ephesians 2:19–22 – The household of God built on the foundation of apostles and prophets.

- Colossians 1:18 – Christ is the head of the body, the Church.

- Hebrews 10:24–25 – Do not neglect meeting together, but encourage one another.

WHAT'S THE POINT?

The Church is not defined by walls or membership rolls but by people transformed by Christ's Spirit. Peter's leadership reminds us that the strength of the Church lies not in perfection but in perseverance. Jesus calls each believer to participate in His ongoing work of building, serving, and proclaiming the gospel.

- How are you contributing to the strength and growth of the Church?

- In what ways can you serve as a 'living stone'—supporting, encouraging, and equipping others?

- How can your faith community better reflect the unity and devotion of the early Church?

- Are you allowing Christ to build His Church in and through you?

FINAL ASSESSMENT:
20-QUESTION MULTIPLE CHOICE TEST

1. What was Peter's original name before Jesus renamed him?

   A. John

   B. Simon

   C. Andrew

   D. James

2. What does the name 'Peter' mean?

   A. Shepherd

   B. Fisher

   C. Rock

   D. Leader

3. Who was Peter's brother, also called by Jesus?

   A. James

   B. John

   C. Andrew

   D. Philip

4. What was Peter's occupation before following Jesus?

   A. Carpenter

   B. Tax Collector

   C. Fisherman

   D. Tentmaker

5. Where did Peter live when Jesus called him?

   A. Nazareth

   B. Bethlehem

   C. Capernaum

   D. Jericho

6. Which miracle first convinced Peter of Jesus' power in Luke 5?

    A. Healing the blind man   B. Calming the storm

    C. The miraculous catch of fish   D. Feeding the 5,000

7. When Peter walked on water, what caused him to sink?

    A. Boat capsized   B. Fear of wind/waves

    C. Jesus pulled him   D. Too far from shore

8. Who revealed to Peter that Jesus was 'the Christ, the Son of the Living God'?

    A. Crowd   B. Andrew

    C. God the Father   D. John the Baptist

9. After Peter confessed Christ, what did Jesus immediately predict about him?

    A. Preach at Pentecost   B. Deny Him three times

    C. Write letters   D. Be a fisherman again

10. How many times did Peter deny Jesus before the rooster crowed?

    A. 1   B. 2

    C. 3   D. 4

11. How did Peter respond after denying Jesus?

    A. Hid in temple
    B. Wept bitterly
    C. Ran to Galilee
    D. Confessed immediately

12. After the resurrection, how many times did Jesus ask Peter, 'Do you love Me?'?

    A. 1
    B. 2
    C. 3
    D. 4

13. What command did Jesus give Peter after restoring him?

    A. Go make disciples
    B. Feed my sheep
    C. Build my temple
    D. Pray without ceasing

14. On Pentecost, how many were saved after Peter's sermon?

    A. 300
    B. 3,000
    C. 5,000
    D. 12,000

15. Who was the first Gentile convert Peter preached to?

    A. Cornelius
    B. Ethiopian eunuch
    C. Lydia
    D. Saul

16. In Acts 3, Peter healed a lame beggar at which location?

    A. Jordan River

    B. Temple gate called Beautiful

    C. Damascus road

    D. Upper room

17. Which NT book describes Peter as a 'pillar' of the church?

    A. Galatians

    B. Romans

    C. Ephesians

    D. Hebrews

18. Which is NOT a theme in Peter's letters?

    A. Hope in suffering

    B. New covenant

    C. Church leadership

    D. Justification by faith apart from works

19. According to tradition, how did Peter die?

    A. Beheaded

    B. Stoned

    C. Crucified upside down

    D. Burned

20. According to 1 Peter 2:5, believers are described as...

    A. Living stones

    B. Soldiers

    C. Fishermen

    D. Priests of the old covenant

ANSWER KEY

1. B – Simon

2. C – Rock

3. C – Andrew

4. C – Fisherman

5. C – Capernaum

6. C – The miraculous catch of fish

7. B – Fear of wind/waves

8. C – God the Father

9. B – Deny Him three times

10. C – 3

11. B – Wept bitterly

12. C – 3

13. B – Feed my sheep

14. B – 3,000

15. A – Cornelius

16. B – Temple gate called Beautiful

17. A – Galatians

18. D – Justification by faith apart from works

19. C – Crucified upside down in Rome

20. A – Living stones

FINAL THOUGHTS

Peter's story reminds you that discipleship is not a single moment but a lifelong journey shaped by grace. From the shores of Galilee, where he first heard Jesus call him, to the city of Rome, where his faith was tested to the end, Peter's life shows that God uses imperfect people to fulfill His perfect will. His path from fisherman to leader of the early Church was marked by courage, weakness, repentance, and renewal.

As you finish this study, remember that the same Spirit who strengthened Peter is at work in you. Every step of your journey, whether through confidence or doubt, success or failure, is an opportunity for God to reveal His transforming power. Let Peter's example inspire you to move beyond past mistakes, receive God's restoration, and walk boldly in your calling. May your life, like his, stand firmly upon Christ, the solid Rock, as a living witness to His grace.

ABOUT THE AUTHORS

Rev. Dr. Shawn P. Richmond serves as Commissioned Ruling Elder / Local Pastor of Prince George's Community Church in Temple Hills, Maryland, and is the founder of Goshen Publishers LLC. Her ministry reflects a deep commitment to teaching, leadership development, and spiritual formation. With a passion for helping believers mature in faith, Dr. Richmond combines pastoral wisdom and academic depth to create studies that are both biblically sound and practical for everyday life. Her work continues to inspire and equip others to live as faithful disciples and effective servants in God's kingdom.

Minister Elder Linda Lee is a devoted teacher, minister, elder, and servant leader at Prince George's Community Church. Her ministry emphasizes Christian education, evangelism, and the mentoring of women in spiritual growth. Through her compassionate leadership and unwavering dedication to God's Word, Elder Lee encourages believers to grow in faith, live with purpose, and serve with humility. Her example continues to strengthen the spiritual life of the church and those she faithfully guides.

www.ingramcontent.com/pod-product-compliance
Lightning Source LLC
LaVergne TN
LVHW051813080426
835513LV00017B/1935